We Have a Latte in Common

Cindy Crosby

Artwork by Anne Keenan Higgins

HARVEST HOUSE™ PUBLISHERS

EUGENE, OREGON

We Have a Latte in Common

Text Copyright © 2003 by Cindy Crosby
Published by Harvest House Publishers
Eugene, Oregon 97402

All artwork is Copyright © Anne Keenan Higgins and may not be reproduced without the artist's permission. For more information about Anne and her work, please contact her at annehiggins@pacbell.net.

Design and production by Koechel Peterson & Associates, Inc., Minneapolis, Minnesota

Harvest House Publishers has made every effort to trace the ownership of all poems and quotes. In the event of a question arising from the use of a quote, we regret any error made and will be pleased to make the necessary correction in future editions of this book.

Cindy Crosby:

For Jeff

Without the patience of my family, this book would not have been possible. Jeff, Dustin, and Jennifer—you're the best! Thanks also to my parents, Bill and Carolyn Strafford, and mom-in-law, Nancy Crosby, for your faith and support. And bless you, dear friends Scott and Vicki Hastings, for first introducing me to the joys of the bean. Thanks also to my writing buddies, Camerin Courtney and Lisa McMinn, for talking shop and offering advice over endless cups of java. Terry Glaspey, Carolyn McCready, Jean Christen, Barb Sherrill, Paul Gossard, and Hope Lyda at Harvest House gave me the opportunity to share my love for coffee in this book, and for this, I'm everlastingly grateful.

As always, thanks to the baristas at Caribou Coffee in Glen Ellyn, Illinois, who let me hang out and write each morning and plied me with some lovely cappuccinos: Daniel, Barb, Sarah, Gemma, Megan, Erika, Megan, Jeff, Liz, Katie, Mallory, Erin, Natalie, Erin, Anne, Nate, Ryan, Jessica, Brian, Julie, and Emily. Hey, folks—thanks for the extra shot of chocolate!

Library of Congress Cataloging-in-Publication Data
Crosby, Cindy, 1961-
We have a latte in common / Cindy Crosby ; illustrations by Anne Keenan Higgins.
  p. cm.
ISBN 0-7369-1074-3 (alk. paper)
1. Female friendship. 2. Coffee—Miscellanea. I. Title.
BF575.F66 C76 2003
248.8'43—dc21

                                                              2002010290

Printed in China.

03 04 05 06 07 / IM / 5 4 3 2 1

To My Friend

_____

With Love

_____

Friendship, like coffee,

is essential to my well-being.

CINDY CROSBY

Getting Beyond the Foam

When you're addicted to cappuccinos, the relationship would seem to be all about the foam. Now true, all that froth is sitting on top of some pretty powerful stuff just waiting to go into action: thick, dark espresso, rich in caffeine and guaranteed to pump the body full of renewed energy. It's like an extra shot of adrenaline, and it's often enough to get you through some work project or problem on the home front. There's nothing like a little help from the bean to kick a tired brain into gear.

But first you have to have the right foam…and oh my, oh my, oh my…the sound of the barista plunging the steam tube into the cold white milk is enough to start me salivating. Skim milk foams the best, they tell me—the lighter the moo-juice, the frothier the suds. It's the best kind of bubbly.

The ideal way to go at it is with a little spoon made expressly for coffee drinks. Slide it across the top, curling just the barest slice of froth onto the utensil, then lick the froth slowly off the sides. MMMMMMmmmm. If your foam is dusted with cocoa powder or chocolate sprinkles, it's even better. A good friend, of course, will call your attention to any chocolate clinging to your lipstick before you head out to run errands.

While you're licking that cocoa and foam off your lips, indulge me for a minute while I break some bad news. Foam doesn't last. It's short-term gratification—the anticipation of something more substantial. Oh, all that creamy froth is a nice *introduction* to the foundational stuff below—the dark, rich, caffeine-filled liquid. But foam is the lightweight prelude to the genuine experience awaiting you right beneath the surface. We're talking *espresso*, girls.

Just as espresso is the foundation of any fine coffee drink, authenticity is the basis of a solid friendship. Now

I'm the first to enjoy a fine gab about the weather or a discussion about the latest bestseller—or to offer my opinion about who makes the best java in town. That's all nice break-the-ice, fluffy, preliminary chit-chat—nothing wrong with that. Most friendships begin with some wonderful foamy moments, and what more delicious, delectable beginning could you ask for? It's a launching point, a foretaste of what's next.

But unless the rapport gets down to the espresso level, I find the friendship tends to melt away into nothingness. Give me the nitty-gritty stuff. I crave rich relationships that stay with me long after the foam is only a sweet memory.

I love how honestly sharing and being vulnerable with you keeps us close. I've got to admit it—at first I figured you'd think less of me when I had that heart-to-heart with you and confided some of my troubles. But I've found that authenticity is truly the caffeine of any relationship—it invigorates, percolates through, filters out the surface chatter, and blends together relationships that last. The friends that stay with you are the best of the beans.

Dropping the "perfect-person" persona leaves me free to be myself so I don't have to work hard to keep up appearances 24/7. My burdens are always a little less heavy when I share them with a girlfriend.

Many of the best friendships I have are built over a cappuccino on the little couch in the corner of my favorite coffee shop. We laugh together, spill troubles, pray about difficulties, and swap stories about the week. The conversation starts off with a little foam, a little creamy surface chatter—just to get things perking. Then, we quickly move past the light stuff that we both know dissolves, and get down to the substantive topics at hand. How are you doing—really? What about that situation with the co-worker? Did you get the lab test back? Have you resolved that issue with your sister?

This means my relationships are not always sweetness and light. Sometimes my espresso friends really tick me off when they shoot straight with me. I start to wonder if I would rather just stick with the frothy white stuff, stay with the surface chatter.

Then common sense kicks in. Okay, give it to me straight. Tell me the truth. I don't want to spend the best moments of my relationship time spooning up foam, even if it is dusted with cocoa. My espresso friends don't "yes" me to death. They take me

to the mat. They hold me accountable. Together, we wrestle with difficult questions about love, life, and faith. We can talk about anything—work, predicaments, family skirmishes.

Espresso is the foundation of any good coffee drink...I mean, relationship. Without the real brew underneath, who needs the foam? I'll take the froth for starters, but for the long haul I want to go deeper. I need the zip and energy—the substance—of my espresso friends. Like you!

Mocha Cooler

INGREDIENTS
1-1/2 ounces chocolate syrup
1 ounce almond syrup
2 shots of espresso
3/4 cup of ice
3-1/2 ounces milk
whipped cream

DIRECTIONS
Combine chocolate syrup,
almond syrup, and espresso
in a blender. Add ice and milk.
Blend until smooth and thick.
Garnish with whipped cream
and a swirl of chocolate syrup.

Your Friendship Adds Flavor

Sometimes I get tired of drinking plain coffee. That caffeinated ambrosia becomes as dull as dishwater. You know—same-old-same-old. What once was something I looked forward to now seems uninspiring and monotonous. Too much of the same thing, day-in, day-out, causes my taste buds to slip into lethargy.

There are some ways around this, and I've tried them all. The easiest thing to do is to add some good things on top. There's nothing like a tower of rich, vanilla-flavored whipped cream to enrich the coffee-drinking experience. When that cold dollop of decadence hits the hot, dark liquid, the resulting combination is the best thing this side of heaven.

A good thing gets even better when you take that whipped/java combo over to the coffeehouse's sprinkle shakers. It's serious decision time. Nutmeg? Cinnamon?

The coffee is prepared in such a way

that it makes those who drink it witty:

at least there is not a single soul who,

on quitting the house, does not believe himself

four times wittier than when he entered it.

MONTESQUIEU

A Coffee Glossary

CAFFE LATTE
Espresso and steamed milk

CAPPUCCINO
Espresso, steamed milk,
and foamed milk

CARAMEL MACCHIATO
Foamed milk marked
with espresso, vanilla,
and caramel

CAFFE MOCHA
Espresso, cocoa, steamed
milk, and whipped cream

CAFFE AMERICANO
Espresso and hot water

ESPRESSO
A highly concentrated coffee
beverage created by
pressurized extraction from
dark roasted and finely
ground coffee

Vanilla sugar? Cocoa powder? A dash or two or three on the whipped cream, and a tired brew takes on a whole new personality. Drop a chocolate-covered espresso bean on the pile-o-whipped, and your old friend joe is unrecognizably splendiferous.

But even with all of these extra touches, I can still find that the coffee under the surface decorations tastes bland. That's when I know it's time to really jazz up my java. I give it a little zest with a flavor shot. A jolt of fruit, a dose of nutty flavor, or a bit of mint brightens up my brew.

Likewise, your friendship perks me up. When my life gets blah, you often pull me out of the doldrums. The special touches you bring to our relationship make me look forward to our times together. You enhance whatever we do—you top it off with rich, rewarding moments. Often there's a bonus—some thoughtful little gift, a card in the mail, or just a word aptly spoken at the right point. A festive touch. You make the ordinary, extraordinary.

Sometimes you add a fruity quality to my day…a shot of cherry, blueberry, raspberry, or banana. Like those knock-knock jokes you tell me, though you often mix up the punch line. No matter. I laugh hysterically anyway. Or the crazy costumes you put together for us to wear to a party—and nobody else is dressed up. Your smile is contagious, your sense of humor outrageous. Our friendship brings me joy.

Other times your friendship gives my life a shot of hazelnut or almond—a little nutty, a little zany. You have a crazy bent toward adventure, toward trying something different. Because you're my friend, you encourage me to experiment with new things, to break out of my mold. Maybe it's attempting a new craft—taking a painting class, joining your scrapbooking club, learning to knit. Or you inspire me to be more courageous, and I take up windsurfing, or learn how to backpack in the wilderness.

Our friendship makes me take risks. I like your moxie.

Then there's the infusion of mint you bring to our relationship—the refreshing, blowing-the-cobwebs-out-of-my-brain kind of flavor. When everything seems stale, you energize me. You prod me out of my lethargy and introduce me to new people. Flipping off the TV, you coax me off the couch to come and have fun. On the spur of the moment, we rent a convertible for the day and drive for hours.

Or we go for a walk together, and you give me new perspective. I see things more clearly, and life regains its zing. You're refreshing.

And don't forget vanilla, even French vanilla. Of all the flavors you add to my life, this is the one I appreciate the most—your calm spirit, your willingness to be there for me. Sometimes I need a friend who just plain listens—quiet and available, willing to sit in companionable silence and drink a cappuccino with me when I don't want advice but still need company. Hard times and good times, up times and down times, you're the basic ingredient, the dependable one who sticks close to me through thick and thin.

You cheer me up. Because of you, my life is unexpectedly rich and flavorful. I get tired of plain coffee, but I never get tired of you. You're my rainbow-flavor friend, my fruity, nutty, refreshing, and just plain best all-around gal-pal, the one I turn to when I need a shot of something different—the one who adds flavor to my life.

 # Time Well-Spent

The problem with expensive coffee drinks is they are just that—expensive. We're not talking affordable here. Think Big Dent In The Monthly Budget. Even if math isn't your strong suit, you can see the dollar signs piling up after a couple days' worth of visits to your favorite coffee shop around the corner…$4.00, $2.56, $3.50. Add a jumbo gourmet muffin or a slice of almond–cherry biscotti to the tab, and you've spent upwards of $20 to $25 per week, easy.

Because my coffee habit is crucial to my well-being, I hoard nickels and dimes, carefully planning for my cherished obsession. Let anyone lay down change on the kitchen countertop and it's mine. (I like to think of this as "liberating" the currency.) The space behind the couch cushions is now a cash-free zone.

Best of all, a coffee-drinking habit is an excuse to buy the Sunday newspaper, in which coupons occasionally appear. Okay, so you have to spend $1.75 to save three bucks. That math I can

do. Plus I get some good reading material to boot.

The wild card in budgeting for coffee drinks is the coffee shop's daily trivia question. Answering it lops a dime off the tab. You never know what question will appear on the chalkboard over the cashier's head: the name of some obscure character on *The Simpsons*; the number of bones in the human hand; the Cubs pitcher who was responsible for the no-hitter last night; or the names of Mother Teresa's children (now that one I got). And of course, the coffee shop has the advantage here—they are asking you to use your brain *before* you've gotten your morning infusion of caffeine! But once in a while, some residual crumb of memory from a long-ago Trivial Pursuit game pops up, and I score the extra ten cents.

Just like budgeting money for coffee is a challenge, budgeting time for my friends is also difficult. It's easy to get caught up in the demands of work and home responsibilities. Sometimes my friends drop through the cracks of my busy schedule.

But friendship, like coffee, is essential to my well-being. Woman does not live by work alone. Using my imagination, I look for little places in my schedule where I can carve out an hour or two. I hoard up lunch dates like pocket change, clear a couple hours to walk in the rain with my best buddy, budget an evening to see a movie— even ditch work for an hour so I can run across town with you and check out that little boutique that just opened.

Time well-spent. I get up an hour earlier and we meet, sleepy-eyed, at the coffee shop to catch up. We plan dinner together, but pick up Chinese takeout so there's no stress in getting ready. My

best friends don't care about my relaxed housekeeping, so we push the stacks of mail off the dining-room table or take our coffee mugs out to the back porch for a good gabfest. Sometimes, I'm sorry to say, my dearest friends like you get the dregs of my energy—the "behind-the-couch-cushions" change. I'll send a short e-mail, throw a note in the snail mail, or pick up the phone for a quick "howya doin'" kind of chat. Even if it's not much, it helps us stay connected. But I try to make this a temporary situation and not let it become a permanent condition.

The bottom line is this—there's nothing cheap about nurturing friendship. I can take a few shortcuts, but there still needs to be an investment made. Life is full of busyness: items to cross off the list, carpools to run, things to do, people to see, places to go. But I want to make time for what's important in my life—coffee and your friendship being two obvious priorities.

Is your friendship worth the time? No trivia question here, and I know the answer even without my morning cup of joe: The good things we save up for usually pay off in ways we can't imagine. So I want you to know this—I'm going to keep looking for any way I can find to budget my time and make our friendship a priority.

Isabel closed her eyes against the morning sun beating on her face. She and Tony sat on a park bench, sipping lattes from carry-out mugs with plastic lids. The thick Sunday Tribune lay between them, its sections still neatly folded in half. Tired from a late night, they had met a short time ago in her hotel lobby, then found a coffee shop on Michigan Avenue. Conversation didn't progress much beyond greetings and coffee decisions as they walked through the quiet streets to Grant Park.

SALLY JOHN
After All These Years

Chicks, Chocolate, and Espresso

We're women who know what we want, at least when it comes to our coffee. Make mine a tall double cappuccino, nonfat, and plenty of foam, please. Maybe you want an extra-large decaf white mocha with a shot of vanilla, heavy on the whip. No hesitation. Although life keeps throwing curveballs at us, with our coffee selections we're confident.

One thing we know we want with our coffee is *chocolate*. What better vice to pair with a coffee indulgence? Sure, a perfectly foamed cappuccino in a white porcelain cup the size of a small bathtub is close to pure bliss. But to be flawless, the foam needs just a sprinkle of cocoa powder on top…okay, maybe a

Ah, that is a perfume
in which I delight;
when they roast coffee
near my house, I hasten to open
the door to take in all the aroma.

Jean-Jacques Rousseau

lot—a *lot*—of cocoa powder. Or even better, chocolate shavings.

Take the espresso bean off the top of your mocha and contemplate it for a moment. By itself, an espresso bean is just your slightly crunchy basic component of a coffee drink. But wrap some chocolate around the bean, and you've got a decorative accessory that's also a treat to eat.

Coffee aficionados appreciate that the best little hole-in-the-wall coffee cafés serve their cappuccino with a little foil-wrapped chocolate candy on the side. It all adds up to this: The only thing that's better than java itself is the double whammy of coffee *and* a little chocolate—swirled in, sprinkled on, or nestled up to the cup, morsel-style.

Our friendship is like coffee and chocolate. We complement each other. The sublime becomes divine. Put us together, and the best things become even better.

We both know what we want in friendship. Together, we look for opportunities to laugh and have fun acting

No coffee can be good in the mouth

that does not first send a sweet

offering of odour to the nostrils.

HENRY WARD BEECHER

slightly outlandish. Other times, we want to cry on each other's shoulders over our messy world that so often brings us to tears. I don't have to always be cheerful and "up" with you—you're not afraid when I'm sad and switch on the waterworks.

It's fun to work on projects with you, whether it's painting the living room in my new apartment or planting flowers outside your new house. We make shared memories that last. Sometimes we help

Good communication
is as stimulating as black coffee,
and just as hard to sleep after.
ANNE MORROW LINDBERGH

each other finish up a big assignment at work where two heads and two pairs of hands are better than one. When it's finished, we know without speaking a word what's next—coffee break!

I like our long conversations over lattes—stirring our drinks as we spill the beans about our week. Faith, family, men, or money—nothing is off limits. With caffeine to jump-start our conversation, we trade ideas, make suggestions, listen sympathetically, and offer each other advice—when it's asked for. We encourage each other to dream…dream big. Our coffee conversations help me make sense of myself and get a better handle on the world.

Remember when I went on that funky diet? You encouraged me to stick with it (small skim decaf latte, please). When you received the big promotion at work, we celebrated (extra-large chocolate-chip mocha, heavy on the whip). Remember the late-night coffee runs to the convenience store when we watched old movies at home and ran out of java? Or the road trips where we carefully checked the map,

The morning cup of coffee has an exhilaration about it

which the cheering influence of the afternoon

or evening cup of tea cannot be expected to reproduce.

OLIVER WENDELL HOLMES SR.

plotting our next coffee "fix"? We'd pull over and enjoy a cup at a local café. Chocolate on the side, of course.

We spend a lot of time together, but your friendship never feels clingy or suffocating to me. You sense the days when I need to be alone, to regroup, to have some down time, and you give me lots of room. I have a margin in which to breathe, space to collect myself. You never smother me.

Our friendship is flexible—never static. It acclimates itself to whatever changes are happening in our lives. In the sultry days of summer, we swap our hot coffee drinks for icy chilled concoctions— coffee ice cream, frozen mocha coolers, iced cappuccinos. Winter means we curl up under our cozy afghans and chat while we flip on the coffeemaker to experiment with brewing and tasting the latest flavors—Mackinaw Island Fudge, Decaf Peppermint Stick, Raspberry Ripple with Almonds. We're not afraid to

Did You Know...?

• The first known coffeehouses originated in Italy around 1645.

• Voltaire was said to drink 50 cups of coffee a day.

• In 1742 Johann Sebastian Bach composed his "Coffee Cantana" to poke fun of Germans' obsession with this liquid libation.

• The first instant coffee was invented by Japanese-American chemist Satori Kato of Chicago in 1901.

• The 1773 Boston Tea Party marked coffee's rise to fame, replacing tea as America's favorite beverage.

try new things, just as we don't worry about our friendship adapting to different phases of our lives.

Tastes change, our lives go off on unexpected tangents, but one thing is for certain—I'll always value your friendship. You are to me as chocolate is to coffee. Your friendship is the little extra bonus that makes my life special.

It was a pleasant café, warm and clean and friendly,
and I hung up my old water-proof on the coat rack to dry
and put my worn and weathered felt hat on the rack above the bench
and ordered a café au lait. The waiter brought it and I took out a notebook
from the pocket of the coat and a pencil and started to write.

ERNEST HEMINGWAY
A Moveable Feast

You're the Best of the Beans

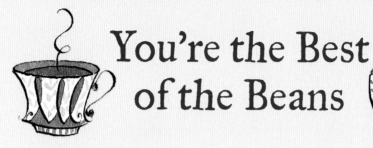

I have to be practical about my coffee choices, but I never settle for second best. There are some hard-and-fast rules. If ground coffee comes in a can the size of a janitorial drum, it's not going to be gourmet. Ditto for those prewrapped hotel filter packs of stale coffee that come in little foil packets. These coffee choices are only for the desperate.

When I choose my coffee, I'm picky. This is a commitment. Okay, a short-term commitment, but an important one all the same. Look for dark beans that are black and oily, guaranteed to give you the most bang for your buck. This is serious stuff. Connecting with the right bag-o-beans will make the coffee experience the stuff of beautiful memories, rather than leave a bitter taste in the mouth.

That's what I love about our friendship. When I picked you,

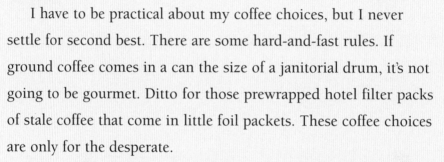

A fig for partridges and quails,

Ye dainties I know nothing of ye;

But on the highest mount in Wales

Would choose in peace to drink my coffee.

JONATHAN SWIFT

it was all about top quality. I didn't settle for second best. Your friendship is gourmet coffee, the real McCoy, the genuine article, bona fide. The best of the best of the best of the best.

I like how we enjoy life together, and that we both have an unspoken allegiance to the bean. When we hit the city for a shopping spree, it's mutually understood that the day will include a few drop-ins at our favorite java locations. Primed by caffeine, we are ready to face the stores. You, as a good friend, are willing to tell me that the lime-green lizard-skin purse might be a teensy bit over the top, and you encourage me to go with the less flashy but more practical bag that becomes my favorite accessory. And I talk you into risking a bit more than choosing the conventional little black dress you pulled off the hanger. We balance each other like espresso and hot steamed milk, or like sugar and cream in black coffee.

Just for fun, we try on shoes and clothes that we know we'll never buy. Balancing a hazelnut latte in one hand, you slip on clunky plastic rainbow-colored clogs with the beaded closures while admiring the snappy fire-engine-red dress shoes with the three-inch heels I put on just for kicks. We both laugh hysterically as we hold up outlandish jumpsuits and sequined jerseys or experiment with oversize sunglasses and say "How do I look?"

If it's a big decision that involves a large outlay of cash, you always know when to encourage me to stop and mull it over before rushing in and making an impulsive selection. Of course, talking over a monumental choice like this calls for some fancy coffee-drinking. There's nothing like a mocha with whipped cream, a sprinkle of chocolate shavings, and an espresso bean to make a person stop and evaluate her options. A mocha can't be gulped down—savoring it slowly while considering a big decision is the way to go.

After an exhausting round of shopping, we collapse in a coffee bar, slip off our shoes, and toast a productive buying day with double cappuccinos. A refreshing jolt of caffeine gives us a second wind. Before leaving, we order Americanos in to-go cups so the drive home will be fueled in the best possible way.

It's not only shopping together. You're comfortable just to talk to. I like hanging out in my kitchen together, talking and trying out some of the latest recipes from our favorite magazines while the tantalizing aroma of just-made coffee permeates the room. We enjoy a cup while baking, basting, broiling, grilling, sautéing, and most of all, talking, talking, talking. We make a batch of cookies to go together with our coffee—and dunk the sugary cutouts into the delicious dark brew.

Sometimes I enjoy our friendship the most when we quietly keep each other company. We both snuggle into comfy armchairs with a pile of new novels and sit together in congenial silence. The only sound is the rustle of flipping pages and the quiet sipping of hot liquid from our favorite tried-and-true coffee mugs. No words necessary, just coffee and companionship. You're such a comfortable person to be with, undemanding and relaxing.

I like sharing my days with you. You're the best of the beans. I love calling you my friend.

If the horseshoe sinks,
then drink it.

OLD CHUCK WAGON
RECIPE FOR COFFEE

Mug Moods

Hold everything! Tell me you're not drinking that perfect caramel mocha out of a *paper* cup. You know the cups I mean— the ones with the little snap-on plastic hat on top and a brown cardboard ring around the middle to keep you from burning your fingers. And don't even *talk* to me about Styrofoam. Not an option for serious coffee drinkers, unless you have exhausted all other alternatives and are in serious need of a fix at a football game or a church potluck.

You can't toast a birthday milestone or a new job promotion with anything that doesn't go "clink." Coffee drinks belong in a ceramic cup for sure—your own being first choice, and the coffee shop's house mug a close runner-up. Never settle for less. If you have to get your brew "to go," pack along a thermal mug created especially to hold the beverage. Your coffee deserves no less.

Q: Why are dark roasted coffee beans more oily?

A: The longer a bean is roasted, the more the natural oils come to the surface.

Last comes the beverage of the Orient shore,

Mocha, far off, the fragrant berries bore.

Taste the dark fluid with a dainty lip,

Digestion waits on pleasure as you sip.

POPE LEO XII

The best little coffee shops encourage you to bring in your favorite mug when you get your daily fix of java. As an incentive, some cafés offer a dime off the total tab—even a bit more if the mug you bring in sports the café's logo.

Of course, you have to be careful what cup you grab out of the kitchen cabinet, lest you disillusion your coffee-shop barista about what a sleek, no-nonsense woman you are. Usually I go with a tasteful mug with some elegant artwork. If I'm feeling especially sassy, I'll pull out one of my mugs with a pithy saying on it. On days when I'm in a hurry, though, I often end up with a mug that looks a little tacky, like the freebie convention mugs that pile up toward the back of the cabinet, or the ones promoting local businesses.

The other day I noticed the barista looking at me a little strangely as she was foaming my milk. When she passed me my cappuccino, I realized I had grabbed the "squirrel dressed as Zorro" mug from the bottom of the cabinet. Oh, well. The body slam to my image was offset by the ten cents I saved.

Some of my friends own beautiful crystal mugs designed to make their coffee-drinking experience an elegant event. (The quality of the coffee automatically ascends several notches just by its proximity to a good beverage holder.) This is not a cup you can swill coffee out of while wearing blue jeans and a T-shirt, however. It requires a certain amount of *savoir faire* to pull off the demeanor demanded by the vessel. It's dress-up, pearls-and-heels, polished-nails, quiet-conversation time.

Other friends take this to extremes. They like to savor their macchiatos out of teensy porcelain demitasse cups. Oversized thimbles. Supposedly, it helps them *focus* on their coffee—"experience" the brew. They inhale the fragrance and take tiny sips, oohing and aahing. These are the same friends who order those fancy meals at restaurants where you get a big plate with one tiny shrimp on it covered with an elegant garnish, or who exclaim over microscopic alpine flowers in their garden—flowers barely visible to the naked eye. As a dedicated, hard-core devotee of the bean, I find that the number

"I relish holding the cup
and savoring the aroma.
It makes me look quite
sophisticated,
don't you think?"

BECKY FREEMAN

of demitasse refills required to bring me to my normal state of caffeinated euphoria is endless. But I humor my friends because I value the relationship (another refill, please).

Don't get me wrong. I'm not averse to beautiful cups and saucers—I just like mine to be at least moderately sized. When I sip black coffee from an old bone-china cup that belonged to my grandmother, it's more than just a coffee-drinking experience. Memories rush in. I become positively sentimental. Drinking coffee from that particular cup and saucer connects me with my family, my past, and my childhood. Okay, truth be told, my budget-conscious grandma always served instant coffee, but it's my memories of her I connect with, not the quality of her beans!

When it comes to serious coffee-drinking, I find my oversized, cobalt-blue hand-thrown pottery mug offers the most slurping satisfaction. It fits my down-to-earth personality. My mug looks lovely and feels comfortable in my hand. When I fill it with hot java, it has just the right weight to it. It's

substantial. The capacity of the mug to hold an ample amount of brew keeps me satisfied and content while I'm chatting with a girlfriend or puzzling over a project.

One of the most comfortable things about our relationship is that you accept me just as I am, no matter what my mood, no matter what "mug" I show you. You know my cheap side, my elegant side, my sassy side, my sentimental side, my sensible side, and even my squirrely side. I don't have to worry which of my "mugs" you see. It's one of the best things about having you for a friend!

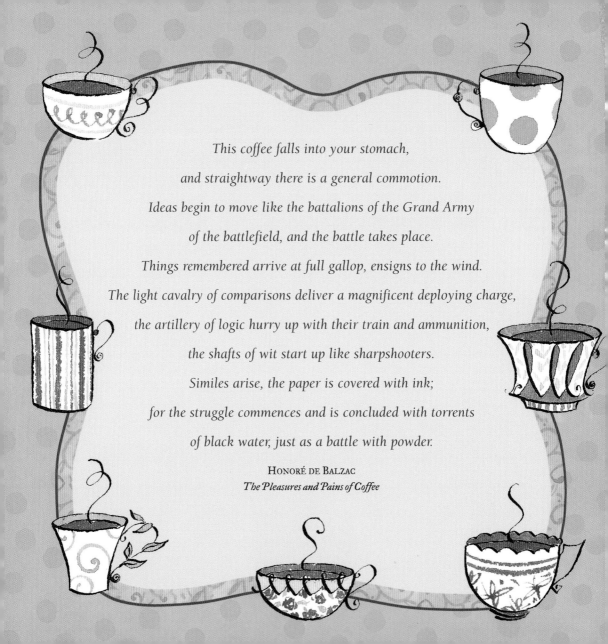

This coffee falls into your stomach,

and straightway there is a general commotion.

Ideas begin to move like the battalions of the Grand Army

of the battlefield, and the battle takes place.

Things remembered arrive at full gallop, ensigns to the wind.

The light cavalry of comparisons deliver a magnificent deploying charge,

the artillery of logic hurry up with their train and ammunition,

the shafts of wit start up like sharpshooters.

Similes arise, the paper is covered with ink;

for the struggle commences and is concluded with torrents

of black water, just as a battle with powder.

HONORÉ DE BALZAC
The Pleasures and Pains of Coffee